Sebastian Currier
Intimations
for Clarinet in B♭ and Piano

BOOSEY & HAWKES

AN IMAGEM COMPANY

DISTRIBUTED BY

HAL•LEONARD®
CORPORATION
7777 W. BLUEMOUND RD. P.O. BOX 13819 MILWAUKEE, WI 53213

www.boosey.com
www.halleonard.com

Published by Boosey & Hawkes, Inc.
229 West 28th Street, 11th Floor
New York NY 10001

www.boosey.com

© Copyright 1989 by Boosey & Hawkes, Inc.
International copyright secured. All rights reserved.

ISMN: 979-0-051-10581-6

First printed 2008
Second printing, computer engraved
Music engraving by Thomas Owen

INTIMATIONS

SEBASTIAN CURRIER

979-0-051-10581-6

Clarinet in B♭

INTIMATIONS
for Clarinet in B♭ and Piano

SEBASTIAN CURRIER

4

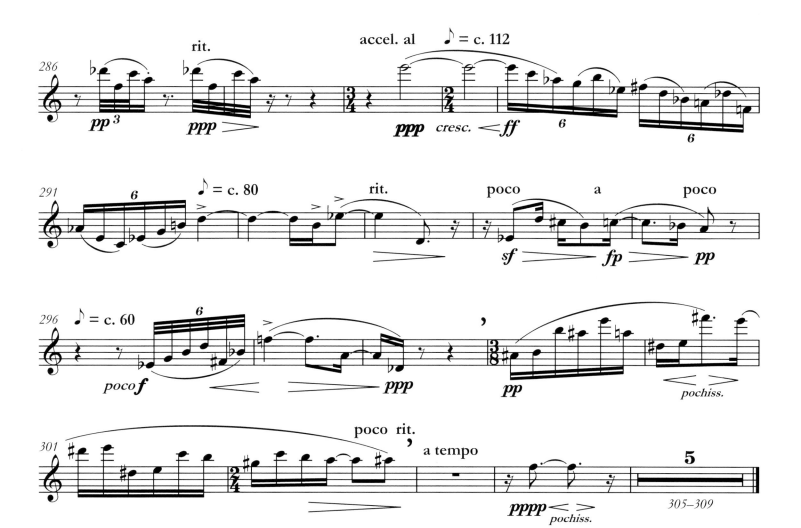

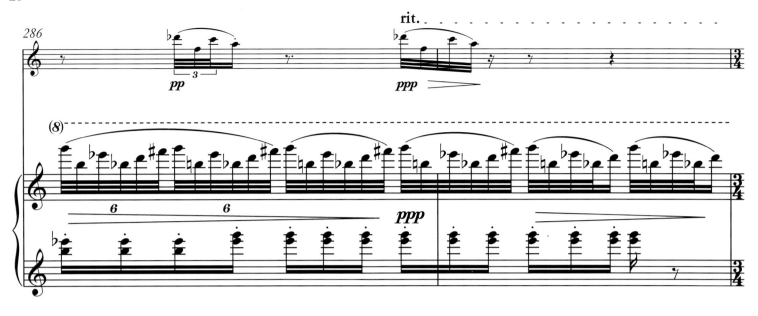

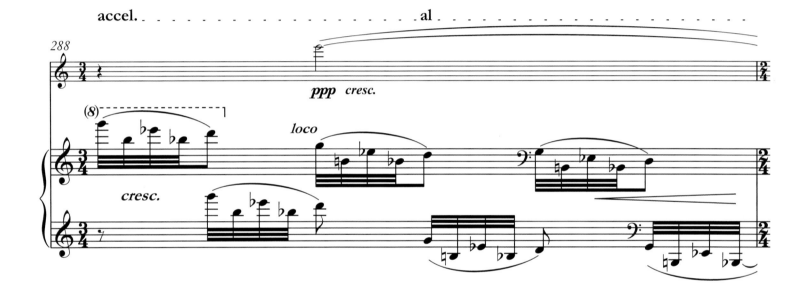

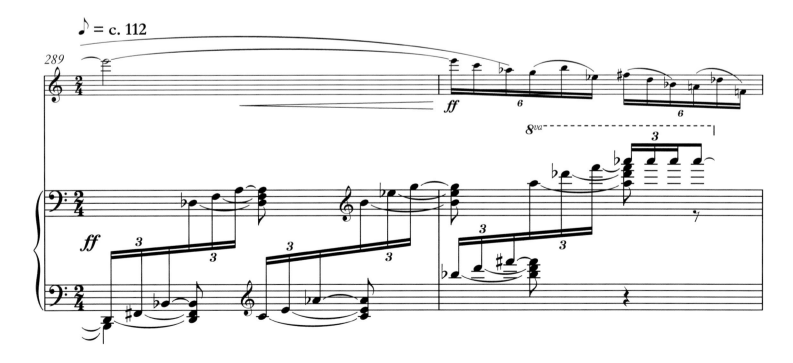

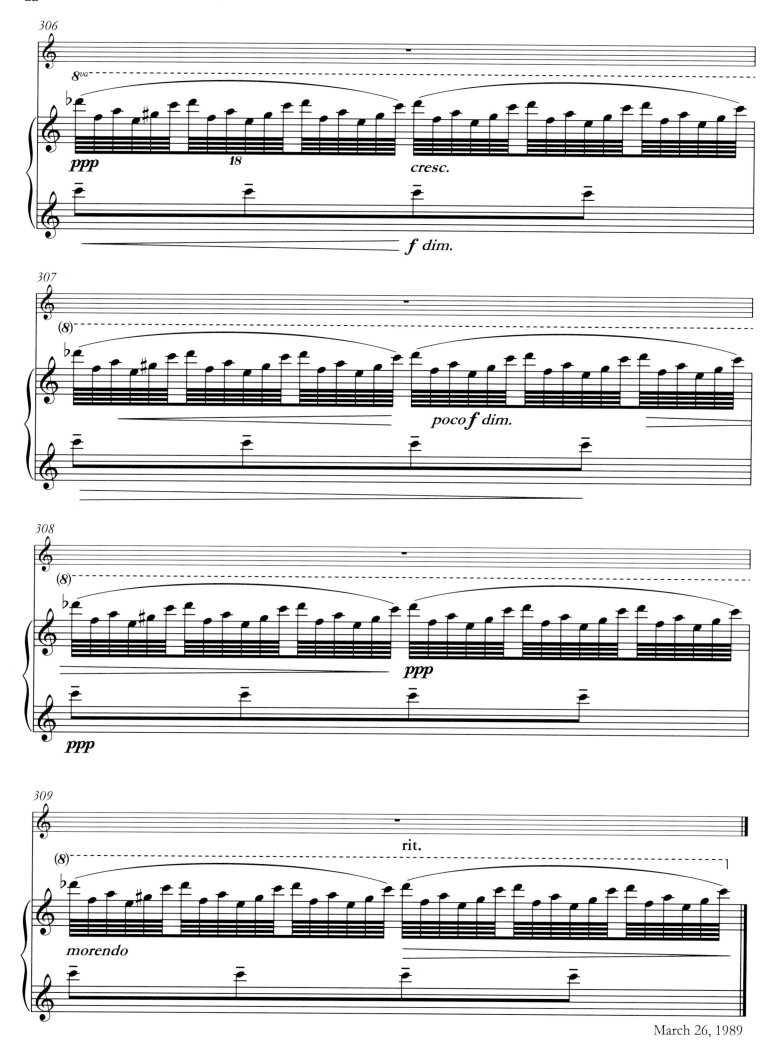

March 26, 1989